Abbey Catholic Primary School, Erdington

Amran Wondemu (6)	1
Reign Rose Tapp (5)	2
Vilte Tinteryte (6)	3
Eldana Asgedom (6)	4
Lace-May Hobbs (5)	5
Bithania Esayasi (5)	6
Yohana Abebe (6)	7
Olivia Keddy (6)	8
James Alphonse Mukalel (5)	9
Nathan Rodrigues	10

Co-Op Academy Smithies Moor, Heckmondwike

Evie Scaife (7)	11
Ruby Alderson (7)	12
Haarush Ankar (7)	13
Joseph Cost (7)	14

Crofton Infants School, Crofton

Eliza Sykes (7)	15
Oliver Leach (7)	16
Leo Staneff (7)	17
Harry Swaine (7)	18
Alessia Horsfall (7)	19
Matilda Croft (7)	20
Nico-Robin Leach (7)	21
Evan Forth (7)	22
Maizie Cleaver (7)	23
Freddie Baker (6)	24
Olivia Birkett (7)	25
Finn Dafoe (7)	26
Arthur Fairbrass (6)	27
Blake Burton (7)	28
Riley Coltman (7)	29
Charlie Burnell (6)	30
Azania Moyo (7)	31
Lana Lemay (6)	32
Aiyla Corp-Khaliq (5)	33
Clara Lawton (6)	34
Olivia Lockett (6)	35
Theodore Psarras (6)	36
Jackson Bibby (5)	37
Elena Hartley (5)	38
William Ellis (6)	39
Millie Hudson-Piper (6)	40
Oliver Evans (6)	41
Rocco Wilkinson (6)	42
Myla Rose (6)	43
Ezra Parker (5)	44
Seren Jarrett-Massey (5)	45
Rae Endeacott (6)	46
Vanshdeep Singh (6)	47
Eloise Mangham (6)	48
Austin Myers (6)	49

Crooksbarn Primary School, Norton

Oliver (5)	50
Leo Butta (5)	51
Halle (6)	52
Ewan Stewart (6)	53
Joey Taylor (6)	54
Hallie (6)	55
Jack Douglas (6)	56
Penny Neary (5)	57
Masha (6)	58

Jaxon Henry (5)	59
Eden Simpson (6)	60
Bobby (6)	61
Flora McFarlane (6)	62
Nancy Johnston (6)	63
Evie (6)	64
James T (6)	65
Alaena Matthewman (6)	66
Matilda Helliwell (7)	67
Rory Groom (6)	68
Daisy Elston (7)	69
Daisy (6)	70
William Gardiner (6)	71
Harriet Waldren (5)	72
Olivia Neary (7)	73
Archie Lumb (6)	74
Amelie Bennett (6)	75
Penelope Kerr (6)	76
Spencer Gell (6)	77
Bea Muir (6)	78
Hunter Kenny (6)	79
Harriette Shepherd (5)	80
Leo Taylor-Hall (7)	81
Nelly Cadwallender (5)	82
Dion Ibrahim (6)	83
Daisy Cowley (5)	84
Bobbi Curwen (6)	85
Tommy Owens (5)	86
Phoebe Butta (5)	87
Arub Sarwar	88
Aydin Taha (6)	89
Lexi (6)	90
Charlie Fewsdale (7)	91

Holbeach Primary School, Catford

Phoebe Marsdon (7)	92
Annie-Molly Ssebuggwawo Blackmore (7)	93
Saatbir Kaur (7)	94
Eliza Da Guia (7)	95
Maggie Hope (7)	96
Khawar Ail (7)	97

Denis Kostadinov (7)	98
Aurora Gardiner-Young (6)	99
Joseph Davidson (7)	100
Ektor Shurbi (6)	101
Sisaaina-Florie Polson (6)	102
Ayden Adesina (6)	103
Etta Jennings (5)	104
Toluwanimi Ajayi (7)	105
Elinor Jobsz (6)	106
Frank Wiremu-Garwood (5)	107
Christabel Bonoh (7)	108
Cecilia Simpson (6)	109
Farhan Idowu (6)	110
Ivo Brooke Yazdi (6)	111
Samuel Mattedi (6)	112
Tia Ocansey (6)	113
Lotus-Imani Abdur-Rahim (5)	114
Arielle Meredith Alcasid (6)	115
Zion McCorkle-Gordon (5)	116
Idris Al-Dasouki (6)	117
Sidney Hackin (5)	118
Gia H (5)	119
Ayo Olukunle (6)	120
Rogan Brown (7)	121
Hunter Lye-Stevens (6)	122
Jo'Nielia Spence (7)	123
Edurne Reyes Cordero (6)	124
Esmé Gani (6)	125
Persis Zacharia (7)	126
Rehan Niazi (6)	127
Omolewa Shobukola (5)	128
Billy N (6)	129
Jad Kanan (5)	130
Adeola Adedoyin (7)	131
Arva Abid (6)	132
Cara Costello (6)	133

Newington Community Primary School, Ramsgate

Hannah Louise Tuffley (7)	134
Jacob Cooper (7)	135
Harvey Thatcher (7)	136
Nelson Drinkwater (7)	137

SENSE
★ POETRY ★

A POCKETFUL OF POEMS

First published in Great Britain in 2025 by:

Young Writers
Remus House
Coltsfoot Drive
Peterborough
PE2 9BF
Telephone: 01733 890066
Website: www.youngwriters.co.uk

All Rights Reserved
Book Design by Ashley Janson
© Copyright Contributors 2025
Softback ISBN 978-1-83685-765-5
Printed and bound in the UK by BookPrintingUK
Website: www.bookprintinguk.com
YB0652E

FOREWORD

Welcome to this book packed full of sights and smells, sounds and tastes!

Young Writers' Sense Poetry competition was specifically designed as a fun introduction to poetry and as a way for children to think about the senses: what these poets can see, taste, smell, touch and hear in the world around them. From this starting point, the poems could be as simple or as elaborate as the writer wanted, using imagination and descriptive language to conjure a multifaceted image of the subject of their writing, rather than concentrating just on what it looks like.

Here at Young Writers, we believe that seeing their work in print will inspire a love of reading and writing and give these young poets the confidence to develop their skills in the future. Poetry is a wonderful way to introduce young children to the idea of rhyme and rhythm and helps learning and development of communication, language and literacy skills.

With poems on a whole range of subjects from animals and everyday objects to emotions and the world around them, these young poets have used their creative writing abilities, sentence structure skills, thoughtful vocabulary and most importantly, their imaginations, to make their poems come alive. I hope you enjoy reading them as much as we have.

Poulton-Le-Sands CE Primary School, Morecambe

Charlotte Arthur (6)	138
Jesse Hales (6)	139
Arlo McGowan (6)	140
Betsy-Alice Brown (6)	141
Isabella Heathday (6)	142
Caitlyn Moffatt (6)	143
Thomas Collier (6)	144
Harper McGowan-Yates (6)	145
John Nowakowski (6)	146
Nyle Liver (6)	147
Ruby Costello (6)	148
Kieran Procter (6)	149
Ava Williams (6)	150
Myla-Rose Munang (6)	151
Betsy Harrison (6)	152
Louis Shaw (6)	153
George Krejcik (6)	154
Eva Topping (6)	155
Anashe Nyika (6)	156
Macie Clement (6)	157
Oliver Whalley (5)	158

Thomas Arnold Primary School, Dagenham

Muhammad Khan (5)	159
Mahdi Abrar Hossain (5)	160
Fatiah Nurudeen (6)	161
Freya Scales (5)	162
Laith Patel (6)	163
Anaya Inayat (6)	164
Jax Mackie (6)	165
Aizah Umar Muhammad (6)	166
Xiangyang Ni (6)	167
Lana Maria Farrell (6)	168
Milana Sosna (6)	169
Kayna Jayswal (6)	170
Sophia Surmachevska (6)	171
Aaila Akram (6)	172
Izabela Gulioiu (5)	173
Mehrish Rahman (6)	174
Kara Breavington (6)	175
Remy Benmore (6)	176
Mason Lovett (6)	177

THE POEMS

The Beach

I can see kids playing in the sea with their parents
I can hear people screaming in happiness
I can smell people eating delicious food
I can feel the soft wavy water
I can taste the scrumptious nuggets and sausages and hot dogs.

Amran Wondemu (6)
Abbey Catholic Primary School, Erdington

Me And Nature, Nature And Me

I can see the sun through the trees
I can hear that birds are near
I can smell the first signs of spring
I can feel the grass tickle my heel
I can taste strawberries and cream, it's so delicious I could scream!

Reign Rose Tapp (5)
Abbey Catholic Primary School, Erdington

Seaside

I can see the sea waves
I can hear seagulls, people and dogs' voices
I can smell the sea smell
I can feel the sand, rocks and water
I can taste my family's picnic food.

Vilte Tinteryte (6)
Abbey Catholic Primary School, Erdington

My Five Senses

I can see the scorching hot sun shining out.
My ears can hear the big loud drum.
I can smell the beautiful flowers.
I can feel the fluffy carpet.
I can taste the icy popsicle.

Eldana Asgedom (6)
Abbey Catholic Primary School, Erdington

The Seaside

I can see the waves going up and down.
I can hear the birds singing.
I can smell fresh air.
I can feel the sand in between my toes.
I can taste ice cream, and fish and chips.

Lace-May Hobbs (5)
Abbey Catholic Primary School, Erdington

Wibbly Wobbly Playground

I can see the long blue slide.
I can hear noise and singing.
I can smell food, coffee and tea.
I can feel pretend cars and different toys.
I can taste burger and chips.

Bithania Esayasi (5)
Abbey Catholic Primary School, Erdington

Spring

I can see trees - they are green
I can hear church songs
I can smell flowers of different kinds
I can feel the air and the sun
I can taste the strawberries and apples.

Yohana Abebe (6)
Abbey Catholic Primary School, Erdington

At The Beach

I can see the bluest sea
I can hear seagulls near
I can smell fish and chips on the pier
I can feel the sand between my toes
I can taste mint ice cream on my nose.

Olivia Keddy (6)
Abbey Catholic Primary School, Erdington

The Beach

I can see the beach and sky
I can hear the waves
I can smell the fish and chips
I can feel the sand
I can taste the ice cream.

James Alphonse Mukalel (5)
Abbey Catholic Primary School, Erdington

Sunny Day

I can see bright sun
I can hear birds singing
I can smell flowers in the garden
I can feel fresh air
I can taste snacks.

Nathan Rodrigues
Abbey Catholic Primary School, Erdington

Competition Day

I can see the beautiful sparkling costumes shining.
I can hear the music playing while people are cheering.
I can smell the hairspray around the room
I can feel the soft, silky pom-poms.
I can taste the hairspray.

Evie Scaife (7)
Co-Op Academy Smithies Moor, Heckmondwike

My Cat, Binkie

I can see her eyes and her fur
I can hear her meowing
I can smell the tuna that she eats
I can feel her soft fur
I can taste when I kiss her, the taste of the tuna coming in my mouth.

Ruby Alderson (7)
Co-Op Academy Smithies Moor, Heckmondwike

Mom

I can see you, my beautiful mom.
I can hear your sweet voice.
I can smell the cupcakes you made, Mom.
I can feel your touch, Mom.
I can taste the cookies you make, Mom.

Haarush Ankar (7)
Co-Op Academy Smithies Moor, Heckmondwike

Sonic

I can see the green emerald
I can hear fireworks
I can smell chilli dogs
I can feel the grass burning
I can taste chilli dogs.

Joseph Cost (7)
Co-Op Academy Smithies Moor, Heckmondwike

Summer

I can see beautiful birds soaring through the cloudless sky.
I can hear the children chatting with excitement about their fun adventures.
I can smell the powerful smell of barbecues.
I can feel excited that summer is finally here!
I can taste strawberry lemonade fizzing in my mouth and ice creams, every flavour.

Eliza Sykes (7)
Crofton Infants School, Crofton

Summer

I can see a symmetrical butterfly flapping in the wind.
I can hear birds tweeting in the endless afternoon sun.
I can smell delicious burgers cooking on a barbecue.
I can feel a warm, gentle breeze blowing on my skin
I can taste an exquisite ice lolly bursting in my mouth, and the fizziness of Fanta Fruit Twist.

Oliver Leach (7)
Crofton Infants School, Crofton

Summertime

I can see children building a humongous sandcastle and playing in the warm sand
I can hear people putting music on under the bright blue sky
I can smell sweet chips and a delicious hamburger
I can feel the golden sand in between my toes
I can taste the Smarties sprinkled on my bubblegum ice cream.

Leo Staneff (7)
Crofton Infants School, Crofton

Summer

I can see the beautiful, cheerful birds singing in the bright green trees.
I can hear the excitement of children playing.
I can smell the delicious smell of a good barbecue.
I can feel the delightful, majestic ice cream in my mouth.
I can taste the sweetness of a strawberry.

Harry Swaine (7)
Crofton Infants School, Crofton

Summer

I can see the colourful, bright sun in the cloudless sky.
I can hear the cheerful songs of birds in the tall trees.
I can smell the wonderful burger from a barbecue.
I can feel the gentle splash of water in the pool.
I can taste the sweetness of refreshing lemonade.

Alessia Horsfall (7)
Crofton Infants School, Crofton

Summer

I can see people having picnics so delightfully.
I can hear children screaming for ice cream.
I can smell crispy barbecues and apples hanging on trees.
I can feel the summer breeze coming towards me.
I can taste pop and candy popping in my mouth.

Matilda Croft (7)
Crofton Infants School, Crofton

A Day At The Beach

I can see people sunbathing in the warm sunlight
I can hear seagulls squawking while they are soaring in the sky
I can smell the salty, deep, blue sea
I can feel the warm, golden sand between my toes
I can taste the delicious ice cream flavours.

Nico-Robin Leach (7)
Crofton Infants School, Crofton

Summertime

I can see lots of glistening shells on the beach
I can hear people diving off diving boards into the glistening water
I can smell the whiff of freshly cut grass
I can feel the slimy seaweed on my hands
I can taste the sugar in ice cream.

Evan Forth (7)
Crofton Infants School, Crofton

Summer

I can see seagulls soaring over the beautiful beach
I can hear the waves crashing into the craggy rocks
I can smell some pizza cooking in the oven
I can feel the hot, golden sand on my feet
I can taste the crunchy sugar on the doughnuts.

Maizie Cleaver (7)
Crofton Infants School, Crofton

Summer

I can see the colourful sun setting over the hills.
I can hear birds singing beautiful songs.
I can smell a wonderful, powerful barbecue.
I can feel the beautiful flowers on my skin.
I can taste the ice pops in summer sunlight.

Freddie Baker (6)
Crofton Infants School, Crofton

Summer

I can see the flowers blooming in the sunlight.
I can hear the songs of birds chirping up in the trees.
I can smell barbecues.
I can feel the gentle breeze blowing on me.
I can taste the sweetness of lollies in my mouth.

Olivia Birkett (7)
Crofton Infants School, Crofton

Summer

I can see the bright sun in the blue sky.
I can hear the cheerful songs of birds.
I can smell the wonderful apples on the trees.
I can feel the sun shining bright at me.
I can taste the delicious apple on the tree.

Finn Dafoe (7)
Crofton Infants School, Crofton

Summer

I can see flying birds up in the colourful sky.
I can hear the trees blowing in the breeze.
I can smell flowers everywhere.
I can feel flowers and the breeze
I can taste the refreshing lemonade in my mouth.

Arthur Fairbrass (6)
Crofton Infants School, Crofton

Summer

I can see birds soaring through the sky.
I can hear birds singing loudly in the trees.
I can smell whiffs of BBQs.
I can feel the gentle waves on my body in the sea.
I can taste strawberries in my mouth.

Blake Burton (7)
Crofton Infants School, Crofton

Summer

I can see beautiful birds in the blossom trees.
I can hear the waves crashing together.
I can smell a pizza cooking.
I can feel the hot soft sand between my toes.
I can taste ice-cold water.

Riley Coltman (7)
Crofton Infants School, Crofton

Summer

I can see birds flying majestically and clouds floating.
I can hear kids playing football and birds chatting.
I can smell a barbecue.
I can feel the texture of steak.
I can taste a sausage.

Charlie Burnell (6)
Crofton Infants School, Crofton

Summer

I can see the sun shining in the sky.
I can hear children chatting.
I can smell a barbecue cooking.
I can feel myself cooling down in the paddling pool.
I can taste cool sweet lemonade.

Azania Moyo (7)
Crofton Infants School, Crofton

Summer

I can see a yellow sun and the blue clear sky.
I can hear people splashing in the pool.
I can smell fish and chips.
I can feel the warm sun.
I can taste cold ice cream.

Lana Lemay (6)
Crofton Infants School, Crofton

Summer

I can see big waves in the sea
I can hear children playing in the garden
I can smell fish and chips
I can feel the warm sun
I can taste ice cream.

Aiyla Corp-Khaliq (5)
Crofton Infants School, Crofton

Summer

I can see the huge blue sky.
I can hear the crashing waves.
I can smell fish and chips.
I can feel the warm breeze.
I can taste yummy doughnuts.

Clara Lawton (6)
Crofton Infants School, Crofton

Summer

I can see flapping butterflies
I can hear buzzing bees
I can smell pollen from flowers
I can feel a wooden fence
I can taste sticky candyfloss.

Olivia Lockett (6)
Crofton Infants School, Crofton

Summer

I can see a golden shining sun.
I can hear seagulls squawking.
I can smell a barbecue.
I can feel a nice cool breeze.
I can taste ice cream.

Theodore Psarras (6)
Crofton Infants School, Crofton

Swimming

I can see transparent water
I can hear excited children
I can smell chlorine in the water
I can feel wet slides
I can taste a hot drink.

Jackson Bibby (5)
Crofton Infants School, Crofton

Park

I can see big swings.
I can hear children playing.
I can smell pretty flowers.
I can feel a slippery slide.
I can taste crunchy apples.

Elena Hartley (5)
Crofton Infants School, Crofton

Seaside

I can see yellow sand
I can hear children playing
I can smell my tasty lunch
I can feel the big blue waves
I can taste yummy ice cream.

William Ellis (6)
Crofton Infants School, Crofton

Summer

I can see the flowers in my garden
I can hear people playing in the pool
I can smell pizza
I can feel the sand
I can taste ice lollies.

Millie Hudson-Piper (6)
Crofton Infants School, Crofton

Blackpool

I can see colourful lights
I can hear loud music
I can smell sweet ice cream
I can feel the hard handrail
I can taste lovely hot dogs.

Oliver Evans (6)
Crofton Infants School, Crofton

Summer

I can see the shining sun.
I can hear waves crashing.
I can smell sun cream.
I can feel the sand under my feet.
I can taste coconut.

Rocco Wilkinson (6)
Crofton Infants School, Crofton

Summer

I can see children play
I can hear butterflies flapping
I can smell a barbecue
I can feel a fluffy dog
I can taste cold ice cream.

Myla Rose (6)
Crofton Infants School, Crofton

Summer

I can see the golden sun.
I can hear children playing.
I can smell barbecues
I can feel a nice cool breeze
I can taste ice cream.

Ezra Parker (5)
Crofton Infants School, Crofton

Park

I can see children playing
I can hear buzzing bees
I can smell sweet flowers
I can feel cool grass
I can taste cold ice cream.

Seren Jarrett-Massey (5)
Crofton Infants School, Crofton

Summer

I can see the hot sun
I can hear quiet birds
I can smell tasty BBQ
I can feel colourful flowers
I can taste yummy ice cream.

Rae Endeacott (6)
Crofton Infants School, Crofton

Park

I can see the fun slide
I can hear children playing
I can smell fresh air
I can feel cotton candy
I can taste sweet candy.

Vanshdeep Singh (6)
Crofton Infants School, Crofton

Butlin's

I can see a roller coaster
I can hear a loud disco
I can smell water
I can feel bumpy beds
I can taste warm hot dogs.

Eloise Mangham (6)
Crofton Infants School, Crofton

Summer

I can see a hot sun
I can hear playing children
I can feel buzzing bees
I can smell hot dogs
I can taste ice cream.

Austin Myers (6)
Crofton Infants School, Crofton

At The Beach

I can see the waves crashing as I sit under the tree.
I can hear the birds tweeting as I sit in the sun.
I can smell the roses growing.
I can feel the soft sand touching my hand.
I can taste lemonade in the shade.

Oliver (5)
Crooksbarn Primary School, Norton

At The Beach

I can see children playing in the pool.
I can hear little tweeting birds that are cool.
I can smell smelly-welly black sand.
I can feel cold water on my hand.
I can taste chips and I like watching the ships.

Leo Butta (5)
Crooksbarn Primary School, Norton

Day At The Beach

I can see waves splashing at the end of the pier as I sit near.
I can hear the trees and bees.
I can smell the roses growing.
I can feel the sand on my hand.
I can taste lemonade while I sit in the shade.

Halle (6)
Crooksbarn Primary School, Norton

One Day At The Beach

I can see the bright sun shining in the sky.
I can hear busy bees buzzing.
I can smell flowers in the salty air as I sit on my chair.
I can feel warm sun on my back.
I can taste a snake in my cake!

Ewan Stewart (6)
Crooksbarn Primary School, Norton

Beach

I can see shells and I ring the bells
I can hear children playing with the ball
I can smell the shiny, bright sand on the ground
I can feel the smooth waves on my feet
I can taste the lemonade.

Joey Taylor (6)
Crooksbarn Primary School, Norton

The Park

I can see slides and rides
I can hear trees and bees
I can smell roses and flowers beside the tower
I can feel the sun on my back, and the flowers
I can taste the lemonade in the shade.

Hallie (6)
Crooksbarn Primary School, Norton

Jacky's Classroom

I can see all the chairs stacked up
I can hear noisy children shouting
I can smell Miss Thomson's smelly feet!
I can feel my head thinking
I can taste fruit from the snack bowl.

Jack Douglas (6)
Crooksbarn Primary School, Norton

The Lonely Snowdrop

I can see snowdrops all around me.
I can hear footsteps when people walk.
I can smell the cold air.
I can feel on me there's air.
I can taste the snow because I ate some of it.

Penny Neary (5)
Crooksbarn Primary School, Norton

The Sun In The Park

I can see children playing on the grass
I can hear birds singing in the trees
I can smell flowers on the grass
I can feel grass on my feet
I can taste lemonade and strawberries.

Masha (6)
Crooksbarn Primary School, Norton

The Mario Park

I can see a zooming roller coaster
I can hear lots of people talking and laughing
I can smell the bread in the toaster
I can feel the tickly grass
I can taste fish and chips.

Jaxon Henry (5)
Crooksbarn Primary School, Norton

Playful Summer

I can see the ice cream man in the van
I can hear singing and bells ringing
I can smell berries and cherries
I can feel sand on my hand
I can taste lollies that taste jolly.

Eden Simpson (6)
Crooksbarn Primary School, Norton

Playful Summer

I can see bees out of the trees
I can hear a lovely long song
I can smell beautiful flowers in rain showers
I can feel sand on my hand
I can taste strawberries and cherries.

Bobby (6)
Crooksbarn Primary School, Norton

Sweet Summer

I can see buzzy bees.
I can hear cars driving on the road
I can smell beautiful flowers in rain showers
I can feel grass on my feet
I can taste summery sweet treats.

Flora McFarlane (6)
Crooksbarn Primary School, Norton

Playful Summer

I can see bees in the tree.
I can hear the waves crashing in the cave.
I can smell a sweet treat.
I can feel the snow on my toes!
I can taste lemonade in the shade.

Nancy Johnston (6)
Crooksbarn Primary School, Norton

Playful Summer

I can see a bee in the tree.
I can hear people walking and talking.
I can smell a sweet treat.
I can feel the breeze on my knees.
I can taste lemonade in the shade.

Evie (6)
Crooksbarn Primary School, Norton

Sweet Summer

I can see fun in the sun
I can hear bees in the trees
I can smell beautiful flowers in rain showers
I can feel the sun on my run
I can taste bolognese, in sun rays.

James T (6)
Crooksbarn Primary School, Norton

Playful Summer

I can see a bird and lemon curd.
I can hear buzzing bees in the trees.
I can smell sweets and treats.
I can feel a cat and a bat.
I can taste honey with a bunny.

Alaena Matthewman (6)
Crooksbarn Primary School, Norton

Playful Summer

I can see a ring on a swing.
I can see a cat scratching the mat.
I can smell the trees in the breeze.
I can feel the sand on my toes.
I can taste a sweet treat.

Matilda Helliwell (7)
Crooksbarn Primary School, Norton

Sunshine

I can see trees in the breeze
I can hear birds singing in the trees
I can smell fish in the dish
I can feel breeze on my feet
I can taste lemonade in the shade.

Rory Groom (6)
Crooksbarn Primary School, Norton

Playful Summer

I can see bats and rats
I can hear moles digging holes
I can smell pretty flowers and rain showers
I can feel fun in the sun
I can taste lemonade in the shade.

Daisy Elston (7)
Crooksbarn Primary School, Norton

At The Beach

I can see children playing on the sand.
I can hear music from the band.
I can smell fish and chips.
I can feel the sun on my head.
I can taste cold ice cream.

Daisy (6)
Crooksbarn Primary School, Norton

Fun Summer

I can see a butterfly in the sky
I can hear trees in the breeze
I can smell treats and sweets
I can feel flowers in rain showers
I can taste cakes and bakes.

William Gardiner (6)
Crooksbarn Primary School, Norton

Under The Sun

I can see birds flying high in the sky.
I can hear the trees here.
I can smell the sweet air.
I can feel the breeze on my knees.
I can taste the sweet cake.

Harriet Waldren (5)
Crooksbarn Primary School, Norton

Playful Summer

I can see holes and goals
I can hear bees in the breeze
I can smell lemonade in the shade
I can feel the breeze on my knees
I can taste sweets and treats.

Olivia Neary (7)
Crooksbarn Primary School, Norton

Musical Summer

I can see the sky up high
I can hear the birds tweeting in the tree
I can smell sweets and treats
I can feel the fun sun on me
I can taste nice ice cream.

Archie Lumb (6)
Crooksbarn Primary School, Norton

Playful Summer

I can see the waves in a cave.
I can hear bees in a tree.
I can smell a sweet treat.
I can feel the breeze on my knees.
I can taste lemonade in the shade.

Amelie Bennett (6)
Crooksbarn Primary School, Norton

The Summer Spirit

I can see birds in the tree
I can hear birds tweeting
I can smell flowers blooming
I can feel the grass tickling my toes
I can taste the summer spirit.

Penelope Kerr (6)
Crooksbarn Primary School, Norton

A Happy Summer

I can see bees in trees
I can hear logs falling on frogs!
I can smell honey that is runny
I can feel sand in my hand
I can taste lemonade that I made.

Spencer Gell (6)
Crooksbarn Primary School, Norton

Cat In A Hat

I can see a cat in a hat
I can hear bees in the breeze
I can smell lemonade in the shade
I can feel sand in my hand
I can taste berries and cherries.

Bea Muir (6)
Crooksbarn Primary School, Norton

Lovely Summer

I can see a cave in the waves
I can hear an ice cream truck
I can smell sweets and treats
I can feel my shoes on the sand
I can taste stretchy pizza.

Hunter Kenny (6)
Crooksbarn Primary School, Norton

Turkey

I can see a big, giant hotel
I can hear birds singing
I can smell Grandma's perfume
I can feel the bedsheets
I can taste the rainbow cherries.

Harriette Shepherd (5)
Crooksbarn Primary School, Norton

Fun Summer

I can see caves and waves
I can hear dogs and frogs
I can smell coffee and toffee
I can feel sun when I run
I can taste berries and cherries.

Leo Taylor-Hall (7)
Crooksbarn Primary School, Norton

The Pool

I can see lots of big waves
I can hear banging, crashing waves
I can smell the chlorine
I can feel water splashing
I can taste soft bubbles.

Nelly Cadwallender (5)
Crooksbarn Primary School, Norton

All About A Garden

I can see a house with windows
I can hear the next-door neighbour screaming
I can smell a flower
I can feel the grass
I can taste barbecue.

Dion Ibrahim (6)
Crooksbarn Primary School, Norton

Garden Butterflies

I can see butterflies are chasing flowers
I can hear bees are on the trees
I can smell mint
I can feel grass curling
I can taste cabbage.

Daisy Cowley (5)
Crooksbarn Primary School, Norton

A Sunny Park

I can see lots of slides.
I can hear very fast rides.
I can smell lots of flowers.
I can feel the tickly rope.
I can taste juicy orange.

Bobbi Curwen (6)
Crooksbarn Primary School, Norton

Butterfly World

I can see twelve big butterflies
I can hear fish splashing
I can smell beautiful breeze
I can feel smooth air
I can taste fresh water.

Tommy Owens (5)
Crooksbarn Primary School, Norton

Under The Sun

I can see the shells and bells
I can hear the birds tweeting in the sky
I can smell food cooking
I can feel my fork
I can taste food.

Phoebe Butta (5)
Crooksbarn Primary School, Norton

Playful Summer

I can see sun fun
I can hear birds singing
I can smell lemonade in the shade
I can feel sand on my feet
I can taste sweet treats.

Arub Sarwar
Crooksbarn Primary School, Norton

The Garden

I can see a ball in a garden.
I can hear some sizzling.
I can smell the BBQ.
I can feel the garden.
I can taste strawberries.

Aydin Taha (6)
Crooksbarn Primary School, Norton

The Bats In The Tree

I can see an owl, I can see cockroaches
I can hear a bat
I can smell blossom
I can feel the bat
I can taste cat biscuits.

Lexi (6)
Crooksbarn Primary School, Norton

Funny Summer

I can see sand
I can hear ducks
I can smell ice cream
I can feel hot
I can taste bolognese.

Charlie Fewsdale (7)
Crooksbarn Primary School, Norton

Christmas Day

I can see a big Christmas tree with pretty, big and small lights, and presents underneath it.
I can hear the choir singing sweetly, as sweet as the nightingale itself. The bells on Santa's reindeer.
I can smell Christmas pudding and mince pies, and the pine trees' foresty smell.
I can feel the hugs from Grandma and Grandpa, tight and warm. I know that I'm safe in their arms. I don't want to say goodbye.
I can taste the chocolates on the tree that they try to hide, but I always find them. Hee, hee!

Phoebe Marsdon (7)
Holbeach Primary School, Catford

Diwali

I can see *beautiful* colours and patterns of rice and powder *and soft and sandy*
I can hear *lovely* music in my ear, sending to the brain, listening to what they say
I can smell *delicious* tandoori chicken that I want to eat
I can feel *bright, beautiful* mehendi patterns, light praised to a clean god or goddess
I can taste *yummy* laddu in my mouth, *crunchy, chewy* in my mouth, some laddu's in there.

Annie-Molly Ssebuggwawo Blackmore (7)
Holbeach Primary School, Catford

My Face, All Nationalities

I can see with my eyes people have different colour eyes
I can hear with my ears some are big and some are small
I can smell with my nose who are different sizes
I can feel with my hands, left and right hands, who also can be different nationalities
I can taste with my mouth and see my lovely white teeth to eat food and fruits.

Saatbir Kaur (7)
Holbeach Primary School, Catford

The Great Fire Of London

I can see fire menacing in the city of London, spreading everywhere
I can hear a church bell ring and people screaming, "Fire! Fire!"
I can smell burning wood and toxic smoke being blown by the strong wind
I can feel that I am about to burn my skin in the blazing fire
I can taste yummy bread given by the people.

Eliza Da Guia (7)
Holbeach Primary School, Catford

Spring

I can see that roses are red, the sky is blue.
You can see me, I can see you.
I can hear birds singing and bells ringing and lots of things like that.
I can smell the awesome blossoms next to me.
I can feel the long grass and the gentle breeze pass.
I can taste extreme ice cream and rich sandwiches.

Maggie Hope (7)
Holbeach Primary School, Catford

Apple

I can see apples in Lewisham fruit market on Saturday.
I can hear the noise of the train passing to Catford Bridge Station.
I can smell apples in a Lidl store.
I can feel the shiny skin of an apple when I eat in Ladywell Park.
I can taste yummy apple when I make apple juice.

Khawar Ail (7)
Holbeach Primary School, Catford

The Beach

I can see the shiny sun, it's time to have fun
I can hear splashing waves, it's a wonderful place
I can smell the salty sea, it's fantastic to be me
I can feel the hot sand, I'm going to be tanned
I can taste the cold ice cream, I'm living the dream.

Denis Kostadinov (7)
Holbeach Primary School, Catford

Summer's Nature

I can see the animals nesting and the birds singing with joy.
I can hear the flowing sounds of bees.
I can smell the sweet smell of lavender in the breeze.
I can feel the hard bark and leaves.
I can taste the cold ice cream as I walk.

Aurora Gardiner-Young (6)
Holbeach Primary School, Catford

Woodland Walk

I can see elegant bluebells swaying in the breeze.
I can hear birds singing amongst the trees.
I can smell the elderflower blooming in the sunshine.
I can feel rough bark trailing against my fingers.
I can taste the fresh spring air.

Joseph Davidson (7)
Holbeach Primary School, Catford

My School, Holbeach

I can see flowers, they are red outside.
I can hear the bell outside, it is loud.
I can smell the water outside.
I can feel the log, the log is hard and it is scrapey.
I can taste the brick, the brick is big in the air.

Ektor Shurbi (6)
Holbeach Primary School, Catford

Our School

I can see recess, screaming for photos.
I can hear people playing, the lunch hall, birds.
I can smell the leaves smell like lemon, and hair.
I can feel flowers, a bench, stairs.
I can taste lemon, cake, pasta.

Sisaaina-Florie Polson (6)
Holbeach Primary School, Catford

Our Five Senses At School

I can see some beautiful flowers growing in the sun.
I can hear some big kids playing happily.
I can smell the food in the lunch hall.
I can feel a hard chair that I am sitting on.
I can taste the air.

Ayden Adesina (6)
Holbeach Primary School, Catford

I Like My School

I can see a big plant pot, a massive building.
I can hear the leaves rustling in the tree.
I can smell the freshener, the yummy lunch.
I can feel hard bricks, a soft carpet.
I can taste yummy fruit.

Etta Jennings (5)
Holbeach Primary School, Catford

Summer

I can see the birds fly up in the sky.
I can hear birds tweeting.
I can smell flowers in the tree.
I can feel the nice green grass.
I can taste the lovely, juicy fruit and ice cream.

Toluwanimi Ajayi (7)
Holbeach Primary School, Catford

My Amazing School

I can see a flower growing in the sunlight.
I can hear children playing in the playground.
I can smell fresh air.
I can feel a soft carpet that is blue.
I can taste delicious fruit.

Elinor Jobsz (6)
Holbeach Primary School, Catford

School

I can see a circular football in the cage.
I can hear the creaky blue door.
I can smell pink flowers in a pot.
I can feel a soft carpet on the ground.
I can taste juicy fruit.

Frank Wiremu-Garwood (5)
Holbeach Primary School, Catford

Senses

I can see a hat on the table.
I can hear music playing on the bed.
I can smell ketchup in the fridge.
I can feel a bag on a suitcase.
I can taste an apple in my mouth.

Christabel Bonoh (7)
Holbeach Primary School, Catford

Sunny

I can see birds flying in the sky smoothly
I can hear robins singing loudly
I can smell lovely flowers
I can feel the warmth of the sun
I can taste the cold ice cream.

Cecilia Simpson (6)
Holbeach Primary School, Catford

Lemon Juice

I can see green and yellow.
I can hear popping bubbles.
I can smell orange.
I can feel squishy. I can feel hard. I can feel bumpy.
I can taste sour. I can taste salt.

Farhan Idowu (6)
Holbeach Primary School, Catford

Lemons

I can see green, yellow segments, white.
I can hear a crunch.
I can smell sugariness, limes.
I can feel slippery, hard, squishy bumps.
I can taste fizziness.

Ivo Brooke Yazdi (6)
Holbeach Primary School, Catford

Our Five Senses At School

I can see very light sun.
I can hear children playing happily.
I can smell very good food.
I can feel soft carpet on the floor.
I can taste very yummy food.

Samuel Mattedi (6)
Holbeach Primary School, Catford

Lemon

I can see yellow, green seeds
I can hear popping, fizzing
I can smell lemon juice like orange
I can feel hard
I can taste sour, sweet, made my face silly.

Tia Ocansey (6)
Holbeach Primary School, Catford

Walk Around Holbeach

I can see big herbs growing in the sun.
I can hear the tap running down.
I can smell lovely lunch.
I can feel bricks.
I can taste orange at playtime.

Lotus-Imani Abdur-Rahim (5)
Holbeach Primary School, Catford

Lemon

I can see yellow, lemon, green
I can hear popping, fizzing
I can smell sour lemon
I can feel hard and spiky
I can taste sour, made my face silly.

Arielle Meredith Alcasid (6)
Holbeach Primary School, Catford

Lemon Man

I can see patterns in the lemon.
I can hear popping sounds.
I can smell fizziness.
I can feel hard and rough bits.
I can taste sour bits.

Zion McCorkle-Gordon (5)
Holbeach Primary School, Catford

Lemon

I can see a round yellow ball
I can hear popping bubbles
I can smell sour
I can feel squishy, soft, slippery
I can taste sour, squishy.

Idris Al-Dasouki (6)
Holbeach Primary School, Catford

Poem

I can see lines shaped like a triangle.
I can hear squelching.
I can smell sour air.
I can feel squishy.
I can taste sourness. A lemon.

Sidney Hackin (5)
Holbeach Primary School, Catford

Poem About Lemons

I can see a ball, yellow dots
I can hear squishy squashy
I can smell sweet and sour
I can feel squishy, soft
I can taste sweet, sour.

Gia H (5)
Holbeach Primary School, Catford

Lemon

I can see lemon, yellow, limes
I can hear popping, fizzing
I can smell sweet, sour
I can feel soft, hard, squishy
I can taste sour.

Ayo Olukunle (6)
Holbeach Primary School, Catford

Looking In Autumn

I can see leaves falling from trees
I can hear running, playing
I can smell pizza
I can feel the ground shaking
I can taste pizza.

Rogan Brown (7)
Holbeach Primary School, Catford

The Fruit Poem

I can see white and yellow.
I can hear bubbling and popping like Coca-Cola.
I can smell sour.
I can feel bumpy.
I can taste sour.

Hunter Lye-Stevens (6)
Holbeach Primary School, Catford

Winter

I can see a white, snowy fox
I can hear soft snow
I can smell Oreo ice cream
I can feel white snow
I can taste Oreo ice cream.

Jo'Nielia Spence (7)
Holbeach Primary School, Catford

My School

I can see a flower near the bench.
I can hear the chirping happily.
I can smell food.
I can feel a flower
I can taste fruit.

Edurne Reyes Cordero (6)
Holbeach Primary School, Catford

My Lemon

I can see banana yellow
I can hear crunching
I can smell sweetness
I can feel hard, like a ball
I can taste sour and sweet.

Esmé Gani (6)
Holbeach Primary School, Catford

My Poem About Snow

I can see snow falling down.
I can hear snow falling down.
I can smell flowers.
I can feel snow.
I can taste strawberry.

Persis Zacharia (7)
Holbeach Primary School, Catford

Lemon

I can see yellow outside and a circle
I can hear popping
I can smell sweet
I can feel hard and squashy
I can taste sour.

Rehan Niazi (6)
Holbeach Primary School, Catford

Teeny

I can see yellow, seeds,
I can hear a crunch,
I can smell sweet,
I can feel hard, soft, bumps,
I can taste sweet, water.

Omolewa Shobukola (5)
Holbeach Primary School, Catford

The World

I can see the chair
I can hear birds whistling
I can smell sunflowers
I can feel pink flowers
I can taste jam sandwich.

Billy N (6)
Holbeach Primary School, Catford

Lemons

I can see a sun
I can hear fizzing like a fizzy drink
I can smell limes
I can feel water
I can taste sour.

Jad Kanan (5)
Holbeach Primary School, Catford

Outside

I can see the sun
I can hear the winds
I can smell the flowers
I can feel grass
I can taste crisps.

Adeola Adedoyin (7)
Holbeach Primary School, Catford

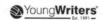

Ten Sour Lemons Jumping On The Bed

I can see yellow dots
I can hear a fizzy drink
I can smell sour
I can feel bumpy
I can taste sour.

Arva Abid (6)
Holbeach Primary School, Catford

Lemony

I can see yellow
I can hear popping
I can smell sour
I can feel hard
I can taste sour.

Cara Costello (6)
Holbeach Primary School, Catford

A Day In Bruges

I can see lots of beautiful chocolate shops on the long, narrow streets.
I can hear the big horses' hooves clickedy-clacking on the bumpy roads.
I can smell warm, sweet waffles and they look amazing, the whiffs go all around the shops.
I can feel the wind and the boat wobbling side to side.
I can taste macarons and they are mango and peach flavour, and they are soft and chewy.

Hannah Louise Tuffley (7)
Newington Community Primary School, Ramsgate

All About The Weather

I can see the clouds in the sky, they're covering the sun. I wonder if it will rain?
I can hear the rain in the distance.
The storm must be coming.
I can smell the wet leaves falling from the trees.
They're landing on the floor.
I can feel the wet grass beneath my feet.
I drink my hot chocolate as it helps me stay warm.

Jacob Cooper (7)
Newington Community Primary School, Ramsgate

Seaside

I can see the big, sparkling, blue sea full of boats.
I can hear the laughter of children having fun.
I can smell fish and chips from the little, lovely fish and chips shop.
I can feel the soft sand, I'm making sand angels with my body.
I can taste soft, creamy ice cream as I sit on the beach, in the sun.

Harvey Thatcher (7)
Newington Community Primary School, Ramsgate

The Amazing Match

I can see the proud, brave players lifting the shiny, gold trophy.
I can hear rowdy fans singing their favourite player. "TJ, TJ, TJ!"
I can smell super delicious chips.
I can feel high fives from my heroes.
I can taste *victory!*

Nelson Drinkwater (7)
Newington Community Primary School, Ramsgate

Summer

I can see rainbow ice cream and pretty flowers.
I can hear noisy seagulls and buzzing bees.
I can smell tasty fish and chips, and lovely sun cream.
I can feel cold sea and crunching sand between my toes.
I can taste yummy ice cream and salty sea.

Charlotte Arthur (6)
Poulton-Le-Sands CE Primary School, Morecambe

Summer

I can see the hot sun and glittering sand.
I can hear children laughing and playing in the sand.
I can smell cheesy burgers and yummy chips.
I can feel the hot sand and the smooth shells.
I can taste yummy hot dogs and good fish.

Jesse Hales (6)
Poulton-Le-Sands CE Primary School, Morecambe

Summer

I can see stripy bees and crashing waves.
I can hear coconuts cracking and crunching sand.
I can smell burning BBQ and spitty sea.
I can feel burning sun and a sharp shell.
I can taste salty air and juicy fruit.

Arlo McGowan (6)
Poulton-Le-Sands CE Primary School, Morecambe

Summer

I can see green palm trees and yellow sand
I can hear the ice cream van and crashing waves
I can smell yummy ice cream
I can feel smooth sand in my toes
I can taste yummy chicken wings and roasted marshmallows.

Betsy-Alice Brown (6)
Poulton-Le-Sands CE Primary School, Morecambe

Summer

I can see melting ice cream and flying seagulls
I can hear waves crashing and bees buzzing
I can smell BBQs and salty chips
I can feel smooth shells and sandcastles
I can taste cold drinks and fruity ice pops.

Isabella Heathday (6)
Poulton-Le-Sands CE Primary School, Morecambe

Summer

I can see yellow sand and blue sea
I can hear squawking seagulls and children giggling
I can smell yummy chocolate ice cream and lovely sun cream
I can feel hard and bumpy shells
I can taste yummy burgers.

Caitlyn Moffatt (6)
Poulton-Le-Sands CE Primary School, Morecambe

Summer

I can see tall ice creams and blue sea
I can hear buzzing bees and crashing waves
I can smell lovely sun cream and burning BBQ
I can feel crunching sand between my toes
I can taste special chicken legs.

Thomas Collier (6)
Poulton-Le-Sands CE Primary School, Morecambe

Summer

I can see soft sand and splashing waves.
I can hear seagulls squawking and bees buzzing.
I can smell salty chips and hot dogs.
I can feel hot sand and the sea.
I can taste lemonade and ice cream.

Harper McGowan-Yates (6)
Poulton-Le-Sands CE Primary School, Morecambe

Summer

I can see brown hairy coconuts
I can hear the ice cream van, squawking seagulls
I can smell yummy fish and chips
I can feel crunching sand under my feet
I can taste juicy orange fruit.

John Nowakowski (6)
Poulton-Le-Sands CE Primary School, Morecambe

Summer

I can see purple flowers and buzzing bees
I can hear children giggling and bees buzzing
I can smell sun cream and salty sea
I can feel the shining sun
I can taste chocolate ice cream.

Nyle Liver (6)
Poulton-Le-Sands CE Primary School, Morecambe

Summer

I can see a big yellow sandcastle and busy bees
I can hear crashing waves
I can smell burnt barbecue and salty sea
I can feel bumpy shells and warm sea
I can taste yummy ice cream.

Ruby Costello (6)
Poulton-Le-Sands CE Primary School, Morecambe

Summer

I can see soft sand and pretty flowers
I can hear waves splashing and seagulls screaming
I can smell BBQ and yummy chips
I can feel the sun touching my head
I can taste burgers.

Kieran Procter (6)
Poulton-Le-Sands CE Primary School, Morecambe

Summer

I can see soft sand and flying birds
I can hear ice cream vans and helicopters
I can smell yummy chips and sun cream
I can feel the smooth sand
I can taste yummy hot dogs.

Ava Williams (6)
Poulton-Le-Sands CE Primary School, Morecambe

Summer

I can see ice cream vans
I can hear a plane in the sky
I can smell nice fish and chips
I can feel the sun on my skin
I can taste cold apple juice.

Myla-Rose Munang (6)
Poulton-Le-Sands CE Primary School, Morecambe

Summer

I can see bees buzzing around.
I can hear waves splashing against the rocks.
I can smell hot dogs.
I can feel sand.
I can taste burgers.

Betsy Harrison (6)
Poulton-Le-Sands CE Primary School, Morecambe

Summer

I can see BBQs and people cooking
I can hear buzzing bees
I can smell fish and chips
I can feel soft sand
I can taste watermelon.

Louis Shaw (6)
Poulton-Le-Sands CE Primary School, Morecambe

Summer

I can see coconut trees
I can hear crashing waves
I can smell fish and chips
I can feel smooth shells
I can taste hot chicken.

George Krejcik (6)
Poulton-Le-Sands CE Primary School, Morecambe

Summer

I can see soft yellow sand.
I can hear waves splashing.
I can smell burning BBQ.
I can feel cold water.
I can taste cupcakes.

Eva Topping (6)
Poulton-Le-Sands CE Primary School, Morecambe

Summer

I can see ice cream
I can hear buzzing bees
I can smell fish and chips
I can feel soft sand
I can taste melting ice cream.

Anashe Nyika (6)
Poulton-Le-Sands CE Primary School, Morecambe

Summer

I can see soft sand
I can hear waves crashing
I can smell BBQs
I can feel hot sand
I can taste bubblegum ice cream.

Macie Clement (6)
Poulton-Le-Sands CE Primary School, Morecambe

Summer

I can see a party!
I can hear the people
I can smell yummy BBQ
I can feel soft, tickly grass
I can taste chocolate.

Oliver Whalley (5)
Poulton-Le-Sands CE Primary School, Morecambe

VE Day

I can see excited people having parties and waving the Union Jack flag,
I can hear VE Day music and people cheering,
I can smell chocolate cake and roasted chicken
I can feel chairs, tables and the Union Jack flag,
I can taste orange juice, Coca-Cola and Fanta.

Muhammad Khan (5)
Thomas Arnold Primary School, Dagenham

VE Day

I can see marching, flags and the royal family.
I can hear fireworks, cheering and music.
I can smell air, perfume, a flower and grass
I can feel kissing, playing drums and hugging,
I can taste Coca-Cola, chicken nuggets, ginger beer and sweets.

Mahdi Abrar Hossain (5)
Thomas Arnold Primary School, Dagenham

VE Day

I can see waving, marching and flags.
I can hear music, cheering and fireworks.
I can smell air, flowers and grass.
I can feel hugging, holding hands and playing drums.
I can taste chocolate, cupcakes and Coca-Cola.

Fatiah Nurudeen (6)
Thomas Arnold Primary School, Dagenham

VE Day

I can see thousands of people come to see the King and Queen,
I can hear music and cheering,
I can smell chocolate cake and vanilla ice cream,
I can feel cuddles and high fives
I can taste smoothies and milkshakes.

Freya Scales (5)
Thomas Arnold Primary School, Dagenham

VE Day

I can see lights, the royal family and flags.
I can hear music, a plane and cheering.
I can smell air, grass and perfume.
I can feel kissing, playing and hugging.
I can taste sweets, jelly and cake.

Laith Patel (6)
Thomas Arnold Primary School, Dagenham

VE Day

I can see the King and Queen and Prime Minister,
I can hear music and shouting,
I can smell chicken and vanilla ice cream,
I can feel the Union Jack flag and hugs,
I can taste biscuit and smoothies.

Anaya Inayat (6)
Thomas Arnold Primary School, Dagenham

VE Day

I can see lights, flags and waving.
I can hear music, a plane and singing.
I can smell air, perfume and food.
I can feel kissing, hugging and holding hands.
I can taste ice cream, jelly and cake.

Jax Mackie (6)
Thomas Arnold Primary School, Dagenham

VE Day

I can see thousands of people and the prime minister,
I can hear music and cheering,
I can smell perfume and cupcakes,
I can feel cuddles and high fives,
I can taste chewing gum and smoothies.

Aizah Umar Muhammad (6)
Thomas Arnold Primary School, Dagenham

VE Day

I can see marching, waving and dancing
I can hear fireworks, singing, shouting.
I can smell a flower and slime.
I can feel kissing and holding hands.
I can taste chicken wings and ice cream.

Xiangyang Ni (6)
Thomas Arnold Primary School, Dagenham

VE Day

I can see the royal family, Buckingham Palace.
I can hear music and crying.
I can smell food and air.
I can feel kissing and hugging.
I can taste macaroni cheese and lemonade.

Lana Maria Farrell (6)
Thomas Arnold Primary School, Dagenham

VE Day

I can see marching and a plane.
I can hear cheering and music.
I can smell air, food and perfume.
I can feel holding hands and kissing.
I can taste chocolate and ice cream.

Milana Sosna (6)
Thomas Arnold Primary School, Dagenham

VE Day

I can see a flag and dancing
I can hear fireworks and cheering
I can smell flowers and perfume
I can feel hugging and holding hands
I can taste ice creams, chips and cake.

Kayna Jayswal (6)
Thomas Arnold Primary School, Dagenham

VE Day

I can see crowds of happy people and flags,
I can hear singing and dancing,
I can smell gum and chicken,
I can feel tables and chairs,
I can taste Fanta.

Sophia Surmachevska (6)
Thomas Arnold Primary School, Dagenham

VE Day

I can see the King and Queen,
I can hear dancing,
I can smell chocolate cake,
I can feel chairs and tables,
I can taste sweets and tea.

Aaila Akram (6)
Thomas Arnold Primary School, Dagenham

VE Day

I can see fireworks and food.
I can hear music.
I can smell food.
I can feel holding hands.
I can taste cake, ice cream.

Izabela Gulioiu (5)
Thomas Arnold Primary School, Dagenham

VE Day

I can see flags, fireworks,
I can hear clapping.
I can smell strawberry.
I can feel hugging,
I can taste burgers.

Mehrish Rahman (6)
Thomas Arnold Primary School, Dagenham

My Sense Poem

I can see marching
I can hear music
I can smell flowers
I can feel touching flowers
I can taste chicken.

Kara Breavington (6)
Thomas Arnold Primary School, Dagenham

VE Day

I can see food,
I can hear singing,
I can smell chocolate,
I can feel hugs,
I can taste cake.

Remy Benmore (6)
Thomas Arnold Primary School, Dagenham

VE Day

I can see waving.
I can hear a plane.
I can smell foods.
I can feel.
I can taste chocolate.

Mason Lovett (6)
Thomas Arnold Primary School, Dagenham

Young Writers Information

We hope you have enjoyed reading this book – and that you will continue to in the coming years.

If you're a young writer who enjoys reading and creative writing, or the parent of an enthusiastic poet or story writer, do visit our website www.youngwriters.co.uk. Here you will find free competitions, workshops and games, as well as recommended reads, a poetry glossary and our blog.

If you would like to order further copies of this book, or any of our other titles, then please give us a call or visit **www.youngwriters.co.uk**.

Young Writers
Remus House
Coltsfoot Drive
Peterborough
PE2 9BF
(01733) 890066
info@youngwriters.co.uk

Join in the conversation!

 YoungWritersUK   YoungWritersCW   youngwriterscw
 youngwriterscw   youngwriterscw-uk

Scan to watch the video!